CW00640897

CLASSIFICATION: POETRY

This book is sold under the condition that it shall not, by way of trade or otherwise, be lent, resold, hired out or otherwise circulated without the publisher's prior consent in any form of binding or cover other than that in which it is published and without a similar condition including this condition being imposed on the subsequent purchaser.

A CIP catalogue record for this book is available from the British Library.

Printed and bound in Great Britain.

Cover photograph of Torquay harbour by Gregory Paul.

ISBN 1-904169-12-0

First published in Great Britain in 2002 by
United Press Ltd
44a St James Street
Burnley
BB11 1NQ
Tel: 01282 459533
Fax: 01282 412679

All Rights Reserved

© Copyright contributors 2002

www.upltd.co.uk

National Poetry Anthology 2002

This anthology features winning entries from an annual competition which is free to enter. Winners also receive a free copy of the anthology. If you would like to enter for next year's anthology, send a loose second class stamp and three poems, each of 20 lines and 160 words maximum, to United Press, 44a St James Street by the annual closing date of June 30th. You can also call us on 01282 459533 or visit our website on upltd.co.uk

Foreword

Selecting all the winners for each year of the National Poetry Anthology takes a lot of time and effort. But unearthing undiscovered gems of poetry makes all that effort worthwhile.

As editor of the National Poetry Anthology since its inception I have to admit that I do have my own personal favourites among the poems in these books.

Oddly enough, it always seems to be that one region produces an exceptionally high standard of poems. It's also odd that it's never the same region.

Again, this year I have my own favourite region from which I think all the entries are truly outstanding. But as poetry is such a subjective thing to judge you will probably read the poems in this year's edition and find that you prefer a totally different area. However, I hope that you will agree with me that the standard this year is as excellent, if not better, than usual.

Peter Quinn, Editor.

❑ **Ann Marsden receives her trophy from United Press Director, Dawn Quinn (left).**

Every year all the winners of the National Poetry Anthology are invited to vote for the best poem in the book. The year 2000 winner was 91-year-old retired teacher Louise Rider of Buckinghamshire and last year's winner was postmistress Ann Marsden from Cleveland for her poem "Take This Aching Heart."

The presentation of the National Poetry Champion 2001 Trophy was made by United Press Director Dawn Quinn. Ann said: "It was a great thrill to be picked as my local winner, but to have so many prizewinning poets vote for me as the National Champion was truly overwhelming." As well as the trophy, which she keeps forever, Ann received £100 worth of books. To find out who was voted as the Champion in this edition, see next year's anthology.

Contents

Each poet listed in this contents of the 2002 National Poetry Anthology is a winner in his or her own right. Their poems were selected as winners for their town or area in a free-to-enter annual competition which featured many thousands of entries. The winners are grouped into various regions. If you do not find a winner from your locality this is because insufficient entries were received from that area.

EAST ANGLIA - Pages 69 - 82

Pam Connellan, Cambridge, Stephanie Polak, Wisbech, Christine Lacey, Willingham, Alistair Morgan, Peterborough, Rosemary Westwell, Ely, J V Sims, Mundesley, Sue Butler, Wymondham, Anna-Louisa Cook, Sea Palling, Barbara Boyer, Newmarket, Keith Tutt, Topcroft, Rebecca Camu, Woodbridge, Richard Stewart, Ipswich.

EAST MIDLANDS - Pages 83 - 104

Les Baynton, Derby, Louise Glasscoe, Buxton, Karen Lumb, Chesterfield, Kelly Whyld, Ripley, Adam Lowe, Loughborough, Mike Preston, Oadby, Shaun Johnson, Melton Mowbray, Derek Taylor, North Hykeham, John Younger, Tealby, Steven Atkin, Utterby, Paul Hughes, Grimsby, Pamela James, Northampton, Simon Arch, Kettering, John Howlett, Daventry, Chris Bulmer, Worksop, Lindsay Merchant, Radcliffe-on-Trent, Veronica Lonergan, Ranskill, Jo Wilkins, West Bridgford, Hilary J Cairns, Retford, Dennis Walker, Oakham.

WEST MIDLANDS - Pages 105 - 120

Clare Harrison, Evesham, Helen Windsor, Barbourne, Yvonne Thompson, Bromsgrove, Paul Portmann, Tenbury Wells, Laurie Clifton-Crick, Pershore, Dorothy Buyers, Oswestry, Don Nixon, Albrighton, Nancy Crosby, Cannock, Sue Hansard, Tamworth, Rita Carter, Warwick, Margaret Bowdler, Leamington Spa, Pat Isiorho, Nuneaton, Ann Flynn, Birmingham, Katherine Parker, Wolverhampton.

NORTH WEST - Pages 121 - 138

Colin McCombe, Moreton, Bernard Gilhooly, Alsager, Clare Button, Chester, Denise Buckley, Ulverston, Julie Varty, Maryport, Mary McManus, Blackburn, Sarah Smithson, Chorley, Jean Emmett, Accrington, Lynn Cooper, Bolton, Veronica Emmott, Firswood, Geoffrey Mills, Oldham, Morag Reid, Birkenhead, Al Pearson, St Helens, Fay Eagle, Prenton, Florence Bullen, Southport, Michelle Wright, Oxton.

NORTH EAST - Pages 139 - 166

Joanne Benford, Hartlepool, Sue Ireland, Stockton-on-Tees, Kevin Leadbitter, Middlesbrough, Doris Green, Darlington, Sharron Bates, Newton Aycliffe, Derrick Hopper, Bishop Auckland, Joanne Thompson, Chester-le-Street, Margaret Brewster, Seaton Sluice, William Osborne, Berwick-on-Tweed, Chris Howorth, Newcastle, Connie Coates, Sunderland, Sue Lozynsky, Bridlington, Mary Wood, Hull, Susan Higgs, Thirsk, Rosamund Hudson, York, Sam Pullia, Sheffield, Tony Noon, Mexborough, Eileen Caiger Gray, Doncaster, Susan Bullman, Castleford, Richard Marshall, Keighley, Natalie Scott, Wakefield, Doreen Brook, Bradford, Miranda Wright, Leeds, Alan Holdsworth, Ilkley, Rachel Jones, Halifax.

WALES - Pages 167 - 178

Patience Musk, Ruthin, Gwyne Carnell, Pontypool, Maggie Smith, Usk, Karen Watkins, Carmarthen, Matthew Plumb, Abergavenny, Michael Dalton, Bridgend, Rhys Morgan, Neath, Gwyneth Pritchard, Caerphilly, Gerald Williams, Cardigan, Guy Fletcher, Cardiff.

NORTHERN IRELAND - Pages 179 - 186

Colin Dardis, Cookstown, Martin Magee, Craigavon, Hazel Wilson, Dundonald, Noel Lindsay, Ballycastle, Beatrice Wilson, Holywood, Noel Spence, Comber.

SCOTLAND - Pages 187 - 195

Laura McLeod, Brechin, Kirk Saunders, Inverness, Theresa O'Hare, Bearsden, Ian Speirs, Kilmarnock, Jack Hastie, Hilbarchan, Leslie Saunders, Edinburgh, May MacKay, Insch, James Adams, Dundee.

South
East

THE MENU

What shall I give my man today?
Something dainty on a tray.
Perhaps I'll use that new pink cloth
And start the meal with chicken broth.
Then lamb cutlets, carrots, peas
Or gammon steaks, they're sure to please.
I've got it - sausage, beans and mash
But then he might like corned beef hash.
There isn't time to do a roast
he might like scrambled eggs on toast.
Perhaps he'd like the salmon roes,
No, that's no good, the cat had those.
And so it's bread and cheese again
He's used to that - he won't complain.

Yvonne D'Arvigny, Bedford, Bedfordshire

NOSTALGIC

Long grasses
nodding gently.
Hum of a bumble bee.
Splash of fish leaping.

Sun hot on my eyelids.
Swish of cows' tails.
Drowsing

Stop the clock
Hold the moment
Wrap me in this time
forever.

Here is completeness.

Lynn Williamson, Kempston, Bedfordshire

THE LABYRINTH

If singing birds and melodious tunes,
Don't strike a chord with your heart.
If your own life and the reality of life,
Seem to be worlds apart.

If you have no good to achieve,
Or no super-objective in life.
If you find your existence not miraculous
But the pain of endless strife.

If you smile outside, but weep inside,
And shed the tears of a clown.
If your hopes and dreams of early youth,
Slowly come tumbling down.

If you can relate to all this numbness,
Which in your soul might be.
And if this is the story of your daily life,
You're just the same as me.

Stewart Harding, Windsor, Berkshire

IM SORE I WAS NOTE

My precious card, "to mum", it read,
Carefully positioned beside my bed.
Those few short words to which I clung
Priceless gift from one so young.
Farewell at last to shouts and tears
How far he'd come in five short years.
All by his own, he worked this art
That made me smile, that warmed my heart,
My little man, you cannot tell
How I shall grieve when you can spell.

Alison Burgess, Newbury, Berkshire

THE LOVE POEM I THOUGHT I'D NEVER WRITE

I look into your own world eyes,
Like a hazel sunset on a tempestuous sky.
Or the moon stinging the waves,
Pure white and silver,
As dusk radiates and I shiver.

I behold you,
That not so pale skin
That glides around your agile, supple, fleshy
being,
That makes me wince and squint from seeing.
Rough-edged perfection that I cannot grapple,
Can't I tempt you to one bite
Of this mediocre apple?
I can sense your alive heart and pulsating blood,
Moving under that yearnful skin I love,
Next to my quiet body, I feel the friction when I
sit with you.
The throbbing of your pulse interrupted by mine,
As your leg grazes past me,
No, I'm not fine.
You can't recognise me palpitating,
We're encompassed by an electric field,
As I've resurrected my defence and stubborn
shield.

Rachel Magdeburg, High Wycombe,
Buckinghamshire

THE STRANGER

She entered in her cloud-like stole.
She seemed to glide o'er the cobbled floor,
And knelt beside the helpless child who writhed
in pain on the cold hard stone,
Her face a mask of purest white,
Her eyes two pools, like darkest night,
She raised her hand to stroke the troubled brow,
The pain was eased,
The anguish now, had left the small childish face
With angelic peace 'twas now replaced,
The figure rose and turned away,
With floating step she went her way, and
Weak men quivered, strong men wept, for the
Beautiful floating figure was "Death".

Irene Robinson, Dagenham, Essex

SPIDER WOMAN

They don't call me spider woman
for nothing; though I'll never spin a web,
not one that's silken anyway

or climb a forty story building
with my limbs changed by radiation,
and my multi x-ray eyes

trained on the thief on the thirty sixth
floor fourth window along.
But when I die,

unable to brush them away,
thousands of small money spiders will
crawl on my skin, build webs in my hair

and launch themselves over
the cliffs of my bones
without care.

Clare Collins, Burnham-on-Crouch, Essex

CELEBRATIONS

Whoever thinks, how much it hurts
to celebrate without a word.

No gifts of love for you,
No pretty gifts for you to adore.
I'll never look into you eyes,
see the love, so full of surprise.

No memories even.
Never had a Mum or Dad to keep these
special days, whenever we meet,
so, I'll pretend,
one day,
the heartache will end.

Ann Stuart, Romford, Essex

THE AGEING CRUSADER

Hate leaves a bitter after taste;
Rage curdles to exhaustion.
Fat and flabby both in body and soul,
I shun the all-encompassing flame
Of more than mere moral indignation.
A spineless reaction to evil
Thus comes the holocaust.
It is not enough to know the differences
Between right and wrong,
One must be counted too.
But now how tiring to keep kicking.
Easier by far to mutter to oneself
With indolent hypocrisy
And sink back into the torpid ashes
Of crusades long abandoned.
Oh for a scouring wind
To dash aside the cup of sour cynicism
And whip these embers into fire again.

Ann T Fletcher, Kirby Cross, Essex

ONLY

Only a dream,
Curling, twisting like smoke, around the contours
of my brain.
Tinged with sadness,
A pain that nestles in corners,
Plaguing, harbouring dread, like some deadly
contagion.

Only love,
Rusty barbs and pulled, slowly and painfully
Out of my bruised and bleeding
Heart, laughing, kissing, and stabbing.

Only blood,
My life's blood, ebbing away,
Hour by hour, day by day,
In this haemophiliac existence,
I slowly bleed to death.

Only death,
The coldness of peace flutters its soft butterfly
wings,
At once beautiful, and cold.
Blank page, empty book,
Tomorrow's hope, waiting, only for nothing.

Only a dream.

Sarah Bidgood, Danbury, Essex

HOME

Everyone a door to somewhere else,
an alien house whose views are something
strange,
to be invited in is to be faced
with eyes to look through that see otherwise.

It's comforting to take a person's life
and craft it lovingly to taste,
fashion it to how it's nice to be
and place it homely where it feels just right.

Yet there remains in loft or attic's niche
that window which throws everything awry,
to reach it is to suffer finding truth
in a vision which won't process till it's mine.

Michael Shearer, Ingatestone, Essex

LIFE CLASS

I place my feet in outlines chalked last week,
I'm lined and crossed like diagrams of beef.
Behind my back I grab the rope and lean,
the figurehead of my glass ship and dream

of slicing icy seas. The waves I break
have tossed them from their easels, I can make
this room an orchard, this dais my warm rock,
become Narcissus, one eye on the clock.

I take it easy on the old chaise-longue,
they've had their tea, the two-bar heater's on.
The tutor's whispered wisdoms will soon cease,
to leave the leaden hush of twelve 6Bs.

I close my eyes. In half an hour we're done,
my babe in my belly, round as the sun.

Nicolette Golding, Woodford Green, Essex

FROM THE FAR SIDE OF 50 ... A JOURNEY

Birth in Gibraltar
that burnt sienna Rock
baboons and traffic scattering the crowd.
Ten was grey-black, world war and London
in ashes stalled in low gear, the night air
shaking.
Twenty was sea green, Boston and babies
new routes at high speed, horn blaring.
At thirty, earth colours, coasting in neutral
treads worn thin, a warning knock inside.
Forty was crimson, throttle wide open
no brakes. Divorce is like that ...

Not far from here stretch the final laps
loom the huge indifferent gods
Now, rushing past September golds
the blues and purples of November
hang beneath each roadside lamp like fog.
It's quiet running and a good December death.
Clean, vast, white on white ahead.

Patricia Crittenden-Bloom, Colchester, Essex

THE AFTER AND BEFORE

Within the smallest heartbeat of a second,
Some unseen hand got up and slammed the door
The simplest tasks took on another meaning,
Your life became the after and before.

The words you'd used so often sounded different.
The laughter that you'd heard and hoped to
share
Was shattered into fragments by the longing
For the laughter that was now no longer there.

Every evening meant tomorrow would be coming
And still the night to bear lay in between.
The only hope, forgetfulness in sleeping,
The agony to recognise a dream.

Elizabeth Cahillane, Petersfield, Hampshire

MET-UNMET

I stand alone, where I should
Stand with you.
Not alongside, but opposite,
Hand in hand, ears attuned
Eyes averted - at least mine.
Heart on sleeve exposed,
And feet on unstable ground
The earth moved, at least for me,
The world no longer the same
As when I met you, when I left.
Like Atlas, we carry the world
And when we change, we change
The world.
Having met you, I am not
Who you met.
I am the one you parted from -
And now unmet.

T B Hennessy, Winchester, Hampshire

SILENT SOUNDS AT AUTUMN'S KNELL

'Twas late summer, the weather so sublime;
Walking around the garden's floral bounds,
It seemed I heard, or felt, autumnal sounds;
Sounds as silent as fallen dew or rime.
Mysteriously, permeating the mind,
I saw petals, fading petals, falling
Gently to earth; their sweet perfume spreading
An ambience, seemingly most refined.
Thoughts then came of shorter days, longer
nights;
A quilted silence with no real ending;
Silver hoar frost's splintered crystals sparkling;
Shadows dappled by sun's reflecting lights.
Then quietly rustling, the leaves they fell,
Blanketing all the earth at autumn's knell.

H Val Horsfall, Knebworth, Hertfordshire

PLACE

There is a place
in the white mountains to the north -
a vast cathedral space.

Within a valley walled by sheer white cliffs,
huge forms of time sculpted stone -
figures - struggling to be men, women -
disembodied gestures.
Frozen in their struggle
as if by some poised and hanging hand,
by some beat,
by an eternally held breath.

This place - where time and change has turned
an inward eye,
into its cool stone heart - is silent,
save for the flutter of doves' wings - from high
above
in their brooding-brows of overhanging rock,
that occasionally ripple the smooth air
and disturb - for a while -
the spirits of strength and silence
that lay sleeping there.

Christopher James Davia, Stevenage,
Hertfordshire

YOUR FINGERS

I feel your cold fingers
on my skin
a slightly greasy sense
that tastes of darkness
in your eyes I see
eternity
in your arms I feel
emptiness
with four black horsemen
we ride to our wedding
dressed in shadows
a veil of sorrow covers my face
Charon leads me to you
and you hold me
till the world darkens
and disappears
you kiss me
and in your eyes I see
my pyre burning

Lise Hvalkof, Broxbourne, Hertfordshire

THE ASSASSIN

To kill and still a tender heart is easy so they say
No need for natural causes nor the unusual
assassin's blade,
Glinting cold in moonlight
Making the bravest feel afraid.

No, surest thrust and easiest kill
goes to the callous lover with so little skill.
For she will never understand the pain wrought
by her thoughtless words,
On he, broken-hearted, at her hand.

How can we guard against such careless bloody
care?
Look not to me for guidance; I've suffered to the
blade.
For it's in man's very nature,
To seek out his "loving maid".

If we can find the answer, it's a treasure we could
sell,
To all the men throughout the land - including
the king as well -
Of how to stop our dear assassin,
From making life a hell.

Robert Barton, Orpington, Kent

FROM THE NORTH DOWNS

Where once the Spitfire coughed and spluttered
High above the patchwork quilt
The trails are gone but the fight goes on
To dismantle what Nature built

Down below on the worn out prairie
The Grim Reaper drives a JCB
To fill our shops with chemical crops
Greens for lunch and cancer for tea

The tractor ploughs its futile furrow
Two miles long, ten thousand years deep
And Euro weeds and title deeds
Are all there'll be next year to reap

Farewell coppice and farewell pasture
We don't need you anymore
Just soulless rows of bungalows
Plastic windows and patio doors

Now spread our hills with sterile theme parks
Packaged fun and Mickey Mouse jobs
Let's pay to see what once was free
So not just once but twice we're robbed

J J Crossley, Egerton, Kent

THE PHOENIX OF ARMAGEDDON

The moon weeps,
his tears unleash legions of unchristened black
doves
to tear apart the eternal stars
stained already by the blood of battling angels.

Trees prise their roots from the sordid earth
and crawl to the seas in endless lines.
It was said that paper lilies still danced and
blossomed there.
Hysterical birds dissolve into the sky like
spreading ink blots.

Grandfathers lay poppies and lukewarm footsteps
in the ashes
as the dark clouds converge like the incense of a
funeral mass.
Embracing only to give a Judas kiss, children
fight
The heavens ache, unconsolable, unforgiven.

No phoenix will resurrect those empty hearts
that loved too little and lived too long.

Katie Weatherstone, Edenbridge, Kent

GRAPES OF WRATH

Stark morning. Commuters march
Brisk from their coffee and boiled eggs.

A man sprawls. His empty legs need new alcohol;
the old
Stinks round his head in a sour aura.

Home was a hefty wife once who squeezed him out,
His ears bruised by arguments and her square fists.

Offers of help. Always the same conclusion:
"This man failed to keep his appointment once
again.
We do not feel he has the motivation to be cured."

Prison, after he left a shop
Wearing six of its overcoats loudly
One on top of another.

Now he swallows his Social Security straight from
the bottle,
Quavers to the day's first off-licence, struts to the
second;
By lunchtime he's joking with strangers,
By dusk his shapeless shadow stirs in a doorway

And his only home now
Is an old, cold newspaper
Pitched in the street.

Mefo Phillips, Faversham, Kent

35

SADNESS

Here everything is quiet
in the snow,

in the water
dripping from the seams of leaves.

Inside I am lying crying
looking out at the white

goose feather sky whose clouds
do not come and go

but stay and stay.
If this is a dream through

some sleep corridor
how would I prefer to wake?

It is only growing seeds for them
to be liquified by cold,

And shadowed by the quickening,
darkening sky gently breathing out

fine shiver of goose down
over my upward-looking eyes.

Jemimah Kuhfeld, Ashford, Kent

THE DEATH OF A VESSEL

Dark mysteries long forgotten
And danger's icy gleam.
The sands hold glories good and bad
And perils ne'er foreseen.

A crushing, breaking crash echoes
On the far distant shore.
A sweeping flock of gulls follow.
A great ship is no more.

Above the deep water of fate,
The moon watches in vain.
Silhouetting a dying ship,
As the sea weeps again.

Emma Chamberlain, Deal, Kent

EMILY

Sunlight streaming through the unblinkered
window.
bare onto white walls,
transforming them from their clinical blankness
for the occasion.
And so the dream-child was born,
delivered into my subconscious crying
the most beautiful sounds from newly expanded
lungs
that spread within her like a butterfly's wings
as she emerges, newly freed from her
womb-cocoon.

Put into my arms still heralding her arrival,
she announces her life in gulping cries.
And you, next to me on the bed,
wrap your arm around us both.
The precious child, now separate,
held on the outside and close,
cushioned differently.

I place her in your arms and she becomes calm at
once, breathing in soft sounds, cooing contentedly.
And I smile, and I think;
how appropriate
that you were the father of the beautiful
dream-child
Who settles so calmly against your body.

Rebecca Burden, Chatham, Kent

SHE

She is no Delia in the kitchen, lives on takeaways
She takes me to the theatre, we see boring plays
She doesn't entertain my politics nor laugh at my
jokes
She doesn't hit the sauce much, but she don't 'alf
smoke
She often works 'til late, comes home sometimes
moody,
She questions why I watch Richard and Judy
She blows a lot of dosh on designer clothes
She grabs the credit card - away she goes
She doesn't like my friends, she says they're no
funsters
She says my family remind her of the Munsters
She is so different to me in so many ways, but
She is my girlfriend and
She is perfect

Nick Oliver, West Norwood, Greater London

UNSPOKEN

You slowly dress a nearby bush as you reveal
an unaccustomed nakedness to every tree.

Together we strip, like peeling old plaster
from healed limbs, skin fresh to the air.

And only our flesh speaks, as if for the first time,
of slow, growing intimacy - a new shyness.

Sharing love on the car blanket, with stone
and shoot beneath, meeting in Brailled sensation,

We are alone together, absorbing impressions,
- the spring-surge of the fingertips.

After, when I ask "what are you thinking?"
it jabs a little, like the root beneath your hips.

Above the trees, a bird makes light
of its love of the sun - repeats its witless calling.

I stroke its rhythm-repetitions, tracing,
on your skin, the words unwritten.

Graham High, Isleworth, Greater London

TIME WELL SPENT

Time is the fire
in which we burn.

Love is the hunter
that stalks us all.

History will attend
to itself.

The heaviest stars live
the shortest of lives
and all suns shine
at various degrees.

As the flames rise higher
remember this;

when sugar burns
it burns bright blue.

Bruce McRae, Kensington, Greater London

SWAN

Like a swan
gliding through time,
calmly, serenely,
leaving V-shaped wake
victorious behind

Yet, underneath
composed exterior
mirrored in life's lake,
frantic paddling
and pedalling
just to stay afloat.

I hide from you
my fears
of losing you.

Robin Adara Lewis, Walthamstow, Greater London

RED EARTH

After we stepped on red earth
without roots walking against
the cold winter
for once realising the distance
created between words heavy
like thick rain
you said no more
on an afternoon like this
with birds heading south
and the park breathing slowly towards
closing time
little remains I think looking at the traces we left
behind.

Ralph Streble, London, Greater London

REMEMBERING YOU

While everyone mourns the loss of 'England's
Rose'
I'll be thinking of you
That scented isle of flowers
Your freshly covered tomb

While everyone decorates great iron gates
An old wound opens, pain penetrates
I'll be laying flowers just for you
I'll be thinking of you

The great are remembered in history books
I'll remember the child without care
The great are remembered for their looks
I'll remember your fair hair

The great are pursued relentlessly
I'll remember you ... the trying years
The great are submerged in publicity
I'll remember you in a tide of tears

I'll remember you, Graham.

Diana Moore, Horton-cum-Studley, Oxfordshire

THOUGHTS ON A TRAIN

As I speed through the tunnel
My thoughts race well ahead.
I've put the past behind me
For just a while, I've said.
But past then catches up with me
and overtakes my brain
A jumbled mass of "if" and "when",
The treadmill once again.

Marie Skinner, Sutton, Surrey

CAT'S EYES

As I gazed at my cat
her eyes grew large,
Huge doors that led to
A distant land.
Fear gripped my heart
But she clawed me through
to be with her in
That distant land.

Now no longer a cat
But my queen was she
I was her pharaoh
And we were as one
In that distant land.

Then the vision faded
And back came we
Through her doorway eyes
From that previous time
When we were as one
In that distant land.

Michael Rowson, Chichester, Sussex

THE WAKING

It is the invisible gap
That tells our love.
It is the way our eyes gaze past each other,
In distinguished silence,
That speaks of our devotions.

It is our hands missing
And gripping invisibility's.
Muttering only the impossible,
That says this is love,
With more certainty
Than the darkness that engulfs me every night.

I will wake up to the sun,
Touching my skin through the window.

I will wake up to you,
Touching me with your words.

Holly Gibbs, Eastbourne, Sussex

TO FLY AGAIN ...

My child, as you leave:
Realise I've done my best,
Raised you, raised you up, often,
And put you down, seldom;

Laughed with you, cried for you,
Pushed and pulled, behind the scenes;
Patted your shoulder, stroked your hair,
Kicked your butt and withstood your "buts";

You know I've paid, oh how I've paid
(Grumpily, with secret rapture);
Do you know how much I've been repaid
With such parental pleasures?

I've answered your "whys"
And made you wise;
Arranged for you to fortify your freedoms
While bashing at my barriers;

So now you go:
Know that we are happy
You've learned to fly again ...

Oh, and remember our number, just in case!

Alan McAlpine Douglas, East Grinstead, Sussex

A SKIN'S FLIGHT

Flurry, exposure to skin
deep shallow edges of blood
dip in
and outside in the rain
a glazed form
walking through the street
looking up at the buildings.

Flurry, exposure to a ruin
of wasted love and suffering
what reason nothing not even
evening will endure

Until I fall to the ceiling
then my legs expanding beyond
location.

I kiss my hands in a last touching
moment between knowing myself
and pitch blackness.

David St Clair, Felpham, Sussex

South
West

THE IMPRISONED GOD

The imprisoned God wears flagstones thin
on his calloused immortal knees,
but answering the prayers of the faithful
keeps his spirits up. Needing no food or drink
he runs up no bills, and the space is vacant,
anyway.
Does he note the jingle of receding keys?
(He could snap the bars of this ageing heart
with his little finger).

Sometimes when my mind is quiet
I hear him singing the anthems he taught me:
'Be valiant, be strong, resist the pow'r of sin!'
that sort of stuff. He doesn't think I hear;
he sings to himself, the way I used to do
when I was his grateful prisoner.

Some mornings on the coast road, queuing in
traffic,
I wind the window down, and watch the furling
waves,
and listen to the surf and seabirds' cries,
and sing with him.

Simon Crowcroft, Jersey, Channel Islands

FRAGMENTS FROM THE FIRE ESCAPE

Below stars that fade into
City streetlight glow,
Thoughts twist amongst smoke;
Iridescent sparks of dreams,
Revelations, memories, skitter
Between blue grey layers.
Words billow into the sky
And descend to cover
Ash specked skin.
Eyes filled with tiredness
Trace the flare and fade
Of orange tinted embers.
Slow track of black down
Smooth flank of cigarette.
Night air cools around us,
Conversation dulls our tongues
But the evening will not
Let us go.

Victoria Old, Bodmin, Cornwall

EMPTY

I am pierced by the light of dawn
Green grass turns grey
Clear skies dull to white
A static wind touches my skin with a morbid air
The sun shines rain,
Nothing is here, crushing something with its
weight,
My body aches to be used,
A dark climax stirs the only passion left.

Adam Matthews, Launceston, Cornwall

POVERTY GLIMPSED FROM A CRASHING JET

I had forgotten them,
forgotten how they looked
and where they lived.
Forgotten their rags,
the ragged animals they kept
and how they smelled of death.
The poor flashed below us,
gaining substance, gaining faces.
Shacks, rubbish and people
fused in a dying flash.

Poor people glimpsed from a crashing jet
never to fly.

Steven Handsaker, Berrynarbor, Devon

THE ROOM, MY UNIVERSE

I lie on my back
in the darkness,
the dark intense black.

Bit by bit, as I open my eyes
shades appear, at first deep greys,
then slightly brighter, shapes:
a coat on a hook
or a figure hanging,
a lion snarling
or a fold in the duvet.

How frightening is the light
as it ferrets round my room.

I spend an eternity here
contemplating the universe.
Sooner or later, it seems,
everything comes to me.
And if it doesn't,
I imagine it so.
Even the darkness
I can dream.

Laurence Shelley, Bideford, Devon

WINDFALLS

From the tree they fall
to the rain-soaked ground,
slowly decaying, turning brown,
once full of colour, vibrant and red,
now slowly drained, to our eyes they are dead.

As for all living things, this is nature's way.
life is given then taken away,
and from death comes rebirth,
and new life springs forth,
as the worlds daily turn nature's natural course,

So why should we fear what we already know?
That as seasons are circles
we come and we go,
and as apples we bloom with
the colour of youth,
and as windfalls we reach the eventual truth,
that existence is fleeting,
a brief interlude,
marking only an end,
and another prelude.

Michael Close, Torquay, Devon

SUBMISSION

She was his love.
Slender, courageous, responsive to his touch,
his sailboat strained at her mooring,
yearning to cast off land-bound shackles.
She was his liberty boat,
her white wings poised for flight.
Released and free to wander,
they'd escape across a dream-sea
where water, wind and waves
would soothe a city-bruised spirit.

He was her love.
A good sea-wife, he'd called her.
A compliment he thought, not knowing.
Confined within the small frail shell, her prison,
Terror and tedium, alternate companions,
consumed her.
The sea, her gaoler, now whispering its menaces,
Slip-slapping the thin hull;
now lashing the cell walls, threatening to engulf.
No more escape to the easy pleasures of
suburban life.

Together they sailed on the ebbing tide.

Susan Martineau, Exmouth, Devon

UP FROM THE DEPTHS

I am battered and worn, a surfer who
has been riding the white-crested waves of sleep
throughout the night, being knocked down into
the muffled blue depths, and then surfacing,
gasping great breaths of salty air.
I push my way through layer upon layer of
foamy sleep, and slowly open eyes crusted shut
with hours spent in the depths of darkness.
Bright yellow sunlight filters through my
half-closed eyes,
and sounds of the summer morning pour in from
outside.
Still drunk with early morning nectar, I lie,
curled up in the soft, warm, whiteness,
stretching and yawning like a new-born child.

Louisa Parker, Lyme Regis, Dorset

MORNING GLORY

The angel of the dawn peeps through my window,
Turning night's black cloak to pearly grey,
Lifting up the blinds, revealing subtle shades.
The promise of another sun-kissed day.
From palest pink, through violet and orange hues
To deepest rose, soft blues and burnished golds.
This is the morning glory at her very best,
As before my eyes a miracle unfolds.
No artist could recapture such perfection.
Nor emulate the changing colour scheme.
Boundless beauty in the eye of the beholder.
Rise with the lark to catch this short-lived dream.
For as the sun emerges from her slumbers
And the moon in opalescence slips away,
It's as though the gates of heaven have been
opened
To admit this magic moment of the day.

Sue MacKenzie, Wimborne, Dorset

TREATMENT

Here
Lies an empty shell,
Its mollusc body gone
Nothing familiar, no sea-smell.

It's cleaned and clinical
After its lemon bath.

It used to be blue, now it's grey
They took its mind away.

I hear these days
It's musical,
A strange and wondrous thing
To hear inside, that sings
So beautifully of memories
And futures and fathoms, oh so deep.

Ah, but I think perchance I dream,
I cannot be quite what I seem.
For sure, I must awake
And go and rest and sleep.

Robin Hilton, Poole, Dorset

STARLING

They ganged up on the power lines all afternoon
Tearaways! Hundred of 'em
Disturbing the peace with their squealing
Then stealing the air space above my home,
Spraying graffiti down walls
Ascending in flock formation,
a wing-clapping chorus
rushing over the rooftop.

Suddenly!
A speeding vandal aims for the open window.
An iridescent ball of black zooms in
showering me with feather confetti.
Wheeling and reeling it drops floorward.
Stunned. Cowering, cornered,
this bully of the bird table
now a fluttering drunk.

In my cupped hands I carry him to freedom,
With a quiver of shining plumage
he sobers up
and is gone.

Jo Astbury, Cheltenham, Gloucestershire

TIME AND TIDE

No sound, no warning
As sky turns black
And millpond sea whips up her fury
With screaming wind
For company.
Leaning against the wind
I struggle homeward, remembering,
I see a child, a loving grandfather
Clasping her hand
While the encroaching sea
Leaps over harbour walls
Cold, grey and roaring
With white spume flying
High tide swirling and meeting
Like retired fishermen at street corners.
Slowly they wade eastwards
Homeward bound.
My body leans against the wind
.... and I remember.

Joan Kingscott, Churchdown, Gloucestershire

I HATE BEING OLD

I hate being old and loathe this decline
I wouldn't allow it were the choice to be mine:
I'd have bodies grow better once "over the hill",
You'd never need medicine or even a pill.
Our limbs would be mobile, nothing would creak;
No-one would think we were old or a freak;
Nobody's hair would ever go white;
There'd be no loss of teeth, of hearing or sight
And one wouldn't grow tired unless it was night.
So when you awoke, you'd feel fit as a flea -
All eager to rise for that first cup of tea.
Days would be hopeful for woman and man,
There'd be no looking wistful, worn out or wan.
Though I know that the ending will come into
play
I'd have everyone leave, all shouting "hooray!"
Departing this earth with a great whoop of joy
"Look out there, I'm coming - HEAVEN AHOY!"

Rita Humphreys, Bridgwater, Somerset

HE PASSES BY

The blind cannot see,
The deaf cannot hear,
Yet they all can show love with a touch.

The dumb cannot speak,
The cripple can't walk,
But they all show their love with a touch.

Then pity the person with eyes bright and clear,
Who moves through his day self-assured,
The person who faces the crowds straight and
tall,
Who has confidence, boldness and nerve.

When there stands the man who is blindest of all
The 'seeing' with eyes blind with strife.
A stumbling, isolate, man on his own.
Who cannot touch people, or life!

We can live if we're blind,
Survive if we're deaf,
And hobble on crutches, not legs.

But the man who can't love,
And the man who can't touch,
Is worth less than the dust out in space.

Wilma Gravenor, Taunton, Somerset

MY GRANDMA

Oh grandmama, what big eyes you have!
Do they help you see all the better
In the dark,
When you're hunting?

Oh grandmama, what big ears you have!
Can you hear,
Your own voice(s)
All the better?

Oh grandmama, what big teeth you have!
Worn sharp by many years gnashing,
And ready,
For a hell of a lot more.

Oh grandmama, what a big nose you have!

No doubt,
If some well meaning person were to gut you
All those you have devoured would emerge,
Singing and dancing.

Thomas Handy, Clevedon, Somerset

HOPE FOR A SMALL MIRACLE ON THE LANE TO BARROW STREET

Stars sharpen round a slice of moon.
Wind wraps a chilly scarf about
my neck. Snow freckles secret lane.
I've shifted something with my boot.

My torch illuminates mud specks
on wintry breast of lifeless thrush
knocked from the sky by speeding truck.
No crossing marked from hedge to bush.

Still warm. A moment since alive.
Its beak is damp. Its eye alight.
I will surrendered wings, "Revive!"
Its legs lie back as if in flight.

Its body soothes my half-numbed hand.
It is not dead. It shall not fall.
A feather's shifting in the wind.
I whisper, "Now! a miracle."

If I have faith, this thrush will break
my cage of fingers, mount a tree
and disregarding cold and dark,
release defiant melody.

Peter Gillott, Warminster, Wiltshire

East
Anglia

IN THE GARDEN CENTRE CAFE

In the garden centre cafe, warm, with pastel walls
and silent floors,
I am the only person under fifty, apart from some
special needs adults
And cheerful girls at the till who greet the
regulars.
Most customers pad in with stiff-legged gait.
Slowly, with interest, they study the cakes.
Beige shoes, stone macs, same perms, checked
slacks,
The men obediently hold the trays while their
wives
Squint keenly for the cleanest table.
The teapots pour badly, the coffee is bitter
And the scones slightly stale, floury in their
mouths
As they chew and gaze sourly into the middle
distance.
Beyond, through the slightly steamed windows,
the hardy shrubs
And the tubs full of primulas bloom and thrive in
the fresh March air.
Fruit trees sway, supple in the breeze.
Spring flowers, sap-full and fragrant, throb with
colour.
Inside the cafe, a papery hand touches the cool
moist leaves
Of a purchased iris with pleasure and delight.

Pam Connellan, Great Shelford, Cambridgeshire

GENUINE CARE

You ask me what I want from you,
You shout, scream and demand
And I wonder how you can be so far away
While remaining close at hand.
We never seem to laugh these days,
We never share a joke.
It would be nice if cruel words didn't come out
Every time you spoke.
Your work's become so important
And I've become less and less,
You ask me what I want from you,
I say try a little tenderness.

Stephanie Polak, Wisbech, Cambridgeshire

THE CRASH

The nightmare was waiting to happen when he
called,
Hi mum, I crashed the car.
Listen to that sweet, sweet sound, he must be
alive,
It's 4 o'clock in the morning, tell me where you
are?
He said he rolled and bounced and rolled again,
The weather's pretty bad up there,
By all accounts it should have been a fatal one,
Yet he walked away, does anybody care?

The madness and the chaos that has been his
life,
Walking on icicles so white,
Brittle moments, knowing he will always survive
Anything now, just come on home tonight,
He cried then, stopped and then he cried again,
How could I give him courage to go on?
Every mother's nightmare became reality,
Yet he walked away, my lucky, lucky son.

Christine Lacey, Willingham, Cambridgeshire

SLIPPING TO SLEEP I DREAMT MY DEATH

Slipping to sleep I dreamt my death
Was not a new beginning -
No tunnel of light to lead me on
With heavenly choir singing;
No judgement there for my dying mind
Saw only an end of knowing -
Heaven was what I was leaving behind,
Not where I was going;
No harp nor halo nor hope in heaven,
No trumpeting angels flying -
All I saw was a ghost of God
At the gates of nothingness, crying.

Alistair Morgan, Peterborough, Cambridgeshire

A CORNER OF ENGLAND

There is a corner of England I see daily from the
train.
A square squat church sunlit cream
behind a mossy mound of spreading plain.

In the centre a tree, a tree of life
Once tall and strong and bold, reaching for the
sky
Now wrenched in two, withered and old
It's large trunk ravaged.
Like a cancer-filled body
It bows - a fossilised monument to the savagery
Of dying.

Horses, dappled, chestnut and grey
preamble gently, nose to the ground.
A deep-dug waterway gushes glistening blue-bell
sounds.

While all else bustles and pushes and strains
Fighting for air in a world of pain
This corner of England remains
a testament to the eternity we seek.
A life that the world knows but rarely reveals.
This, our corner - our England.

Rosemary Westwell, Ely, Cambridgeshire

THE EXILE

Last night I dreamt of England, and once more
felt the chill -
Of soft caressing snow flakes, saw ice upon the
rill.
Then I saw tall trees sprinkled with a web of pale
green lace,
And heard a cuckoo calling from its secret hiding
place.

Admiring their reflections in a pool did willows
weep,
And I saw soft and misty hills and valleys still
asleep.
Flower decked meadows bright and gay, a lark on
soaring wings,
And candles on the chestnut trees, and fruits
that summer brings.

The grey stoned church I knew so well, the sheep
among the graves,
The hidden place where badgers dwell, the
sheltered hillside caves.
How often in my thoughts I stray along the
well-remembered way,
How many times have I in memory seen, the
places I have left behind,
The places I can only find in memories, or
sometimes in a dream.

J V Sims, Mundesley, Norfolk

ON THE TROLLEY-BUS TO KIROVSKY ZAVOD

A fat man with a large red dragon
tattooed on his forearm
enquires politely if I am from a Baltic Republic.
No I tell him, from Norwich,
flattered not to be thought Western.
My friend has been to Norwich, he says,
he found it uncomfortably crowded,
a lot like Venus, only dirtier.
His friend is from Mars,
which is much like St. Petersburg
with wide rivers and European architecture.
I ask if on Mars people have to queue.
he says of course ... don't they everywhere?
But what is really amazing
is that the women go naked,
never sleep or menstruate,
bathroom taps gush ice cold vodka
and on Mars the trolley-buses are free.

Sue Butler, Wymondham, Norfolk

THE CALL OF FIRE

His lips brush tentatively against mine,
A first fading echo of summer's wine;
Burning fire courses down through my scorched veins,
Drawing closer, relinquishing my pains;
Drowning deep each other's stains.

Gentle touch, large hand against neck and cheek
Transmits through caress more than he could speak;
Utterance unsaid of complete respect,
A tender desire, no more to deflect;
Emotions pool and collect.

Inadequately expressed beyond words,
He, the fiercely-sweet melody of birds,
Leaves my soul tingling, lips loudly ringing;
Walking away, my heart won't stop singing;
Not able to stop grinning.

Not ever before has this felt so right,
Through joy and all peace, and sobbing at night;
Not ever before, never quite like this,
An awakening of such
Sweet sweet fire given by my lover's kiss.

Anna-Louisa Cook, Sea Palling, Norfolk

SHORT STOP

To write about
a train
without sounding naff
Put it down
if you're bored
I won't be annoyed
In fact, I don't think
I can do it!
So here's where it stops
We're at the station
Everyone off.

Barbara Boyer, Newmarket, Suffolk

LOVE SONNET

Is it enough that I should carry bags of stuff?
Or do the washing-up on time?
When all the while I dream of climbing crags,
White water rafting and a life of crime.
Confused by what you want or just pretend
I lead a life divided into two:
Will superman today his white shirt rend,
Unveil his pants and come to rescue you?
Or, looking at the weather, take my drill
And think about the list of things to do.
Then offer up my well-honed skill
And penetrate the walls to honour you.
In the pale bathroom I will build a shelf
There, in a bottle, I shall keep my Self.

Keith Tutt, Topcroft, Suffolk

STATUS QUO

In the worldly tank
fish people mouth agreements
Their bubbles blow upwards
and burst on the surface
being no subject for scrutiny.

Oh fish people are
free
thinkers
even as they eddy around
all four corners
of their square world.

Rebecca Camu, Babingham, Woodbridge, Suffolk

STRATFORD ST MARY

These long, jointed pipes
Straddling the brown stubble
Are threading their way, doubtless.
To hidden crops needing the benison
Of cool water, except that here,
At the fracture, that same gift
Is wasted on spent land.

All night I lay by the gushing water
Watching the long procession of women,
Tall, elegant dark-skinned women,
Soft footed on the night's stillness
Stooping low to fill their vessels
With the gift of cool, continuous water,
Threading their way in and out of my dreams.

Richard Stewart, Ipswich, Suffolk

East
Midlands

ELECTRONERD IN LOVE

I sent you erotic E-Mail
hard copy filled with sin,
Now I'm waiting on my web-site
For you to zap right in

You've got a really cute little mouse
And your floppy discs are gorgeous,
Your hypertext is just the best......
My hard-disc has grown enormous

I just want to span your electronics
Gaze into your Windows 98,
We'll even meet your motherboard
My CD Rom's in such a state

Come and read my Webzine
Get your search engine on my line,
Passion.co.you and me.
We'll be electro fine

Together we'll Yahoo through the night
Sail to Altavista with each other
You won't care when I corrupt your files
Cos you'll always be my cyber lover

Les Baynton, Littleover, Derby, Derbyshire

HER SELF

The mantle of her sickness
hung about her shoulders
like a shawl. Her cough boiled,
her knuckles were tight and gnarled.
She crocheted silence
fingering every loop.
The moon on her clock face rose.

Louise Glasscoe, Buxton, Derbyshire

SMILE

Life is like a camera
FLASH and every second
Immortalised on the
Negative of your soul.

The lens never scratches
The picture never fades
Printed memories for
The gallery of your mind.

Vibrant colours survive
The changes in time.
CLICK the counter
Winds continuously.

No need to change the
Film, no need to change
The batteries. An everlasting
Album of your life.

Each moment
Recorded, picture perfect
So SMILE for the camera.
Laugh for the day.

Karen Lumb, Chesterfield, Derbyshire

MISERY

Misery is with me tonight.
It is pacing the room
Back and forth
back and forth.
I keep covering my ears
to its loud footsteps,
keep burying my head in the pillow
to block out its screams.
It is yelling in my face,
yelling words I cannot comprehend.
How so bland an emotion
can rant and rave like this,
I do not know, but
it is tearing through my room
like a spoilt child,
competing with the rage
of the wind outside.
The storm deafens me.
All night long my misery talks
and will not let me sleep.

Kelly Whyld, Ripley, Derbyshire

SAVIOUR OF THE FALLEN ONE

When the night is dark, and I feel lost and alone,
When I feel I've no one left to call my own,
You wipe the tears from my cheeks,
And carry me home.

When the pain is so great I cannot stand,
You remain strong and reach out your hand,
I'm a drowning sailor,
And you are the land.

And through this life there are bad times and
good,
Days of bright sunshine, and nights drenched in
blood,
But you kept me alive,
And I knew that you could.

Adam Lowe, Loughborough, Leicestershire

DRIVING TO WORK

When I drive to work,
I go the long way round so that I can pass
hedgerows
and drive beneath the boughs of trees
and see hills
and animals in fields
and great white clouds against pacific blue sky.

As I step out of the car,
remove my shoes and socks and run down to the
sea,
I realise I've missed my turning.

I phone in sick, sitting on a donkey.

Mike Preston, Oadby, Leicestershire

LINEAR

I watch a programme on a television screen
before looking through the front room window
and watching as people pass.
The world has become linear,
as flat as a blank piece of paper.
The porcelain figure of a white-haired boy,
on a shelf above the radiator,
has become indistinguishable from the picture in
the catalogue you bought it from.
I look in the mirror
before studying my hand.
I cannot tell the dimensional difference.
I am not sure which is which anymore.

Shaun Johnson, Melton Mowbray, Leicestershire

A RURAL LAMENT

The valley mourns the passing of the trains;
Hoots and trails of steam abound no more;
No passengers wait with chickens in crates
For the clanking signal and level crossing gates,
And the slamming of the third class carriage
door.

Dappled meadows luxuriate in peace,
Horses crop, cattle chew their cud.
Villagers wait for a bus that's always late;
Platforms and track are abandoned to their fate;
A "pottery" is proclaimed where once the station
stood.

A gaudy tractor weaves brown corduroy;
A heron stalks a lively lisping stream;
In single file, ramblers tilt at a crooked stile,
At a crumbling bridge lean and rest awhile,
Where railway navvies used to sit and dream.

Today came strangers sporting yellow helmets,
Whose stilty theodolites must tally.
Bulldozers will follow, levelling every hump and
hollow;
And villagers grumble as through mud they
wallow.
Then behold! A motorway across the valley!

Derek Taylor, North Hykeham, Lincolnshire

COMING HOME

We kept them in the war -
Rhode Island Red, Minorca Black,
White Wyandott and Plymouth grey
to amplify our rations.
But I disliked their scaly legs,
sly cluckings, shifty eyes
and readiness to mob the weak.
Left to themselves, they scattered,
then every dusk came drifting back.

Red cruelty, black lies,
white rage and grey betrayal -
sins of the intervening years -
feel ugly as those long-dead fowls.
I fear as much their manic cackle,
knowing eyes and scratchy feathers,
the gouge of beak and claw:
everything you'd rather not remember -
come home, at last, to roost.

John Younger, Tealby, Lincolnshire

ANIMAL FOOD

Cows stand in the fields of plenty
gentle timid creatures, born to die
in the name of the traditional Sunday roast,
and the steak and kidney pie.

Luckier they than the fowl in the battery,
who never see daylight or hatch their eggs.
carved into nibbles and nuggets and chunks
and the colonel's savoury legs.

Pigs executed for bacon and ham.
The young calf slaughtered for veal.
Stripped of their skin and bleeding flesh.
Their carcasses ground down for meal.

Liver and kidney, tongue and brain,
torn from the gut of the beast.
Sausages, tripe, sweet meats, black pudding.
Gentlemen, come to the feast.

Our food, our clothing. Our shoes and our soap.
We parade in their fur and their hide
while the sun shines down on the fields of plenty,
and on man, with God on his side.

Steven Atkin, Utterby, Lincolnshire

BY MY FIRE

There he sleeps by my fire
What secrets are locked in his mind?
Secrets of peace I admire.
A knowledge known well by his kind.

Can he read me with his amber eyes?
Can he see my thoughts with their gaze?
How can he have a stare so wise,
And instinctively know all my ways?

Does he ever dream of a wolf clan?
Is the warmth just some meagre bribe
To hold him in service of man?
Has he turned his back on his tribe?

Or does he still pulse with wildness?
Does he dream of forests and snow?
Why does he treat man with such mildness,
When man was his deadliest foe?

This wolf who sleeps by my fire.
What secrets are locked in his mind?
The secrets to which I aspire,
The peace that I cannot find.

Paul Hughes, Grimsby, Lincolnshire

THE TERRACOTTA POT

Earth fired,
it holds the heat of Tuscany,
the memory of oil and wine,
a summertime
of silver and of gold.

It holds
a cache of sunflower seeds,
ripe olives
shaken from September trees
on gentle hills.

And deeper still
there lies a wealth of days
and sunshine filtered through
a haze
of happy years.

Pamela James, Northampton, Northamptonshire

LONG STORY

familiar faces
ask me how
I've been
and out of habit
I say *Oh fine*
then realise
I can't lie
and say things
could be better
curiosity stirred
but I shake
my head
Long story

Simon P Arch, Kettering, Northamptonshire

THE URBAN MORNING CHORUS

The night-jar of the milkman,
The keening car alarm.
The hooting of the revellers return.
The twittering of the lonely wife
as her mate departs at dawn
screeching off to catch the morning train.
The boom of the big motorbike
and the rattle of the old diesels
Waking up the baby
Cot-bound and full of grizzles.
The greetings of the dawn-light friends
as they call from kerb to kerb.
It's the urban morning chorus
that does nothing but disturb.

John Howlett, Daventry, Northamptonshire

THE CLOCK TICKS ON

As the blood empties from his veins
The grass grows red beneath his hand.
The slow hands of the clock move on
With measured ticking, mimicked by
The pumping of his weakened heart.

No footprints will he leave again.
His brain, no longer functioning.
The perspiration hugs his brow.
Too late to turn, too great the hurt.
His destination never reached.

He must stay here beneath the bough,
The clear sky dappled through the tree.
This man, about to meet his God
No longer bleeds, for he is dead.
He goes nowhere. The clock ticks on.

Chris Bulmer, Worksop, Nottinghamshire

ISLAND LIFE

Nobody seems to notice that
I'm smiling with worried eyes
That my features betray my feelings
That I'm lonely inside of this clever disguise
A crowd of blank faces
With painted smiles
This inebriated gaggle
tirelessly treading the tiles
In truth are we sharing
The same empty ache,
just pretending we're happy
for each others sake?
This superficial life
now I'm seeing more clearly
is sapping my spirit
leaving me weary
This playground paradise
a paradise lost
Surrounded by beauty
but at what cost?

Lindsay Merchant, Radcliffe-on-Trent,
Nottinghamshire

TOMORROW'S

Today, I met a child
To whose imaginings no glass, nor door could
prove effective barrier
He told not a tale from tightened lips or
distracted hand
Yet bade me, as audience.
Come listen, come learn, come fly.

Today, I met a child
To whose reasonings no adult mind with bonds
and bounds might conjoin
She spoke not a word midst thoughtful confusion
and meditated simplicity
Yet taught me to soar with the wind.

Tomorrow, I'll fly
With wings outspread to touch the inner child
With innocence worn as one would a golden cloak
And leaving behind the weight of years in nested
warmth
I too will soar, momentarily,
Youthfully,
Once more.

Veronica Lonergan, Ranskill, Nottinghamshire

AWAKENED MEMORY

He touched my cheek with tenderness;
I slapped his hand away.
How could he know of his offence
Or what he did that day?

No insult or vicious word he spoke
Could turn me from him more
Than to rest his foreign, unlicensed fingers
Where you had touched before.

Jo Wilkins, West Bridgford, Nottinghamshire

SLEEP WILL NOT COME

Sleep will not come. I've tried all night.
I've tossed and turned but cannot quite
Find that elusive thing called sleep;
So many times I've counted sheep
But that has failed to ease my plight.

All hopes of sleep have taken flight
I am exhausted and despite
My efforts to abstain, I weep;
Sleep will not come.

I see the early morning light,
I do not have the strength to fight;
I so much crave a slumber deep,
This uphill journey is too steep.
I've given up. Try as I might,
Sleep will not come.

Hilary J Cairns, Retford, Nottinghamshire

VULGARIA

What constitutes Vulgaria?
Plastic fish in aquaria
Or is it stretch motor scooter
Flag bedecked with triple hooter?
Table dancing to Oompah band
Umbrella cocktail in your hand.
Ghastly magnets on fridge door.
Collecting beer mats by the score.
Exotic wedding with bridesmaids
In crop tops and designer shades
And as accessory to those
Multi-coloured stilettoes.
There can be nothing scarier
Than falling victim to Vulgaria.

Dennis Walker, Oakham, Rutland

West Midlands

A PLEA AFTER DWELLING ON THE PROSPECT OF LIVING ALONE

Let's book a day to die,
So we never say goodbye.
No tears down a lonely face,
no memories or empty space.

Let's book a day to die,
So we can take off and fly.
Souls forever with fingers laced,
Our eternity firmly embraced.

Let's book a day to die.
So we never have to cry,
The tears of a grieving widow
Who can't and won't let go.

Please, let's book a day to die.

Clare Harrison, Evesham, Worcestershire

ODE TO DEATH

Fading like wind
softly, slowly,
caressing, enticing.
Fingers entwined,
guiding, deciding.
Darkness becomes light,
blindness becomes sight
as the reaper calls collect.

the reaper in all his glory,
the reaper in all his splendour,
his touch true,
so lustfully tender.

Whispering, seducing,
bones become fluid,
flowing,
tempting.

The reaper in all his glory,
the reaper in all his splendour
his touch true, tender.

I surrender.

Helen Windsor, Barbourne, Worcester,
Worcestershire

ON GETTING OLD

The alternative's worse, they say.
Well, of course it is.
But this option has its drawbacks.
Nothing is what it was
And the girl inside your head
Is an old woman on the outside.
The sexual appraisal in men's eyes
Is replaced by indifference or
At best (or worst?) a kindly pity.

Yvonne Thompson, Bromsgrove, Worcestershire

RIVER SCENE

Early morning mists
caress the distant hills
and the church steeple
is in silhouette,
pointing sharply upwards
like a rocket to be launched.
The wide river lies before me,
black and forbidding,
yet the sun's rays
have stabbed its centre
in a swarm
of sparkling pools,
each pool
a separate mirror of light.

The morning lifts its veil
as a lone figure
walks along the towpath
and slowly stirs
the stillness of the hour.

Paul Portmann, Tenbury Wells, Worcestershire

ISLANDS

What shall we do today, my dears,
When black crows blow in the overcoat sky?
Toss Autumn leaves to the warm, grey wind
And gather the chestnuts lying by?
Or sail to the lands of tamarind
Through hurricanes and crocodiles
To the dreaming shores of distant isles
With murmuring surf for our lullaby?

When the door swings idle in the empty hall,
Oh tell me, what shall we do today?
Is it time to seek or time to hide?
Shall we ring the bell and run away?
Or will the whispering walls confide
That life is short, recall hereafter
There is no record of our laughter,
And only love does not decay.

For at the end,
When the tides rise, my dears,
We are all ourselves islands
Surrounded by our tears.

Laurie Clifton-Crick, Wick, Pershore,
Worcestershire

LAMENT

Lord, what is my life become
When there is no growth,
Only the worn root
And the wasting leaf -
No flower, no fruit?

Jewels of light
Tremble in the sea,
Like dewdrops in the fields
Of the dawn,
But my soul is dark.

Love has never come to me
Entirely, in one piece,
But shattered,
Like the reflections of the moon
In the night sea.

Dorothy Buyers, Oswestry, Shropshire

REFLECTIONS

For one moment, she turned her little head,
Lips curving in a crinkling smile at me,
Her eyes the greyness of a Northern sea.
She laughed out loud at something I had said.
The sound pierced through the barriers of years,
Stabbing scar tissue, memory's carapace.
Again I glimpsed that long forgotten face,
Suddenly felt the sting of held back tears
Shed silently behind a bedroom door;
The sharp stiletto thrust of grief again,
That gaping loss of when she died, But then
It passed. My daughter smiled at me once more.
I laughed too. For reflected in that smile
My mother lived again a little while.

Don Nixon, Albrighton, Shropshire

MAY TIME

What a beautiful month is the month of May,
The evenings get lighter and the sun shines all
day
The trees dressed in blossom of pretty pink and
white,
The birds are singing from morning till night,
The colourful gardens, all kinds of spring flowers,
Made ever more lovely by a few gentle showers,
Little lambs skipping in the fields oh so green,
And wild rabbits scampering trying not to be
seen,
There's nowhere on earth I am happy to say,
Than an English countryside in the month of
May.

Nancy Crosby, Cannock, Staffordshire

JENNY

She's still my Jenny
yet not my Jenny anymore.
Her face is disappearing
deep into her skull,
her personality
fading
fading into the pillow.

I was not prepared for this
to hold silent vigil
at my daughter's side,
to watch
and watch her
slow leaving.

Still, I dare not leave
nor seek respite
from this soul-pain
borne on every breath
and sigh
wordless prelude
to her last goodbye.

Sue Hansard, Tamworth, Staffordshire

REUNION

One was dead, the other waiting.
We knew it would happen,
The doctors had said so.
Before it did, I was consoled,
With a dream.
They were running together.
Fast and easily, down a grassy road.
Faster, faster they ran,
Glancing at each other excitedly,
With all the power of youth.
And then they were free.
In the air, above the road,
Birds they became.
Their union was complete.
Their spirits flying,
Their souls free.
No more pain
No more separation.
Happy and together
For all eternity.

Rita Carter, Warwick, Warwickshire

EMBRYO

Something started to go wrong
Were you too soon after
The creation of another
A brother?
Better not to be born
Than deformity make your life unbearable.

Joining all creation's
Unfinished business:
Pupae that never became
Butterflies,
Frogspawn that lies all spring among the weeds
And never succeeds
Beyond that stage.
Eggs grown cold within the nest.

It was 'for the best'
Did you have a spirit?
I only know you did inherit
Love.

Margaret Bowdler, Leamington Spa, Warwickshire

TIME TO LEAVE

I sit alone under the clock without hands or face
Stripped bare of the right to show personal
emotions
Just to keep peaceful oceans,
But am I merely tearing the lace
From my existence until no meaning remains
And the will to live drains
Slowly away without anyone caring a damn?
I know I should leave
If I am to keep my worth as a person,
Yet here I am
Living within a restricting sleeve
Of oppression with my humanity all but gone.
I should shave the edge off my anger
Let the bitter bristles fall to the floor,
Get the decision made
And head for the door.

Pat Isiorho, Nuneaton, Warwickshire

SKIPS

I go skipping in the dark;
I coined the phrase from a deep pocket.
A roomy craft like a jubilant sun
Has docked on my street, uplifting faces.
I peel a layer, survey like a magpie,
Duck into a shoal of segments, haul a plant
From remnants that cling like reptiles,
Carry a portly pot to an airy room,
Blow on wilting leaves
Like a life-guard giving mouth to mouth;
Send soothing messages. The shrub has soared;
Tell-tale tremors keep me pouring.

Ann Flynn, Birmingham, West Midlands

YESTERDAY

I only have to set eyes on you
and that's good enough for me
the overcliff's winding path
leading down towards the sea
sunlight shimmering onto a turquoise surface
waves racing towards the shore
it's wonderful to journey back
to this place once more
golden expanses of sand
stretching as far as the eye can see
past reminders, so heavenly
I can't but help daydreaming
whilst I simply stare
what became of the child upon that beach
now but a shadow with golden hair?

Katherine Parker, Wolverhampton, West Midlands

North West

WONDERLAND OF WINTER

I love this brumal landscape,
The night time of the year.
When morn is dressed in silvery garb
And the air is crisp and clear

The way the frosted grasses stand
Decked out in winter jewels
While bulrushes stand, bedraggled
Trapped in ice bound pools.

Like ice topped cakes the hedgerows stand
Capped white, rich browns below
And here and there a rose hip shines
In pale December's glow.

Yes I love this winter landscape
With its colour and tannic smells
With its grizzled fields of corduroy
As the year bids its farewells.

Colin McCombe, Moreton, Cheshire

THE CROWN

Under the new-risen sun
The young tree hears the song
Of new life through her branches run;
With her gentle green
She covers, unseen,
Thorns that are growing sharp and long,
In spring
To crown a king.

Bernard Gilhooly, Alsager, Cheshire

SOMEWHERE BEYOND

The drizzle makes the pavement shimmer,
Fume sour rain collects on concrete plains
A ragged child stands alone;
She watches traffic and faces flicker past
They are both mere fragments to her.
She stands and stays as if not existing
Shrouded by the city's damp and rottenness
Her face rendered grey by the world's weight.
She is more woman than child, it seems
Past recollections, future hopes fatally wounded
By broken fortune's shards.
Dreams stifled like a scream in the night.
She is insignificant among the bleary buildings
Rotting yet monastic in the rain.
She knows there is a silence somewhere beyond
the noise
Beckoning yet unreachable through the city's
barbed talons
She wants to dream, but knows it's not allowed,
She turns, her careworn shoes wheezing,
The rain watches her walk away
Then forgets she was ever there at all.

Clare Button, Chester, Cheshire

WHAT IS A POEM?

A poem ...
is a cluster of words
that flow and twist
and gently turn
into a parody of people, places
a forest of social happenings
and graces.
Poems are glowing
with a flourishing spectre,
a dream, a vision,
an inspiring collector
of trees,
of morning sun and storm
that collage and weld together
to form ...
A poem

Denise Buckley, Ulverston, Cumbria

EVERGREEN

Never no more will the trees touch our heavens,
And all because we would not learn our lessons,
Of days gone by, when trees were plenty,
A place for everything in its place,
A time when the earth was green and never
empty,
A purpose for being here that's being undone,
In the land where trees once stood.

Julie Varty, Maryport, Cumbria

IF ONLY FOR A NIGHT

Let me drown in your complexities
If only for a night,
and step outside of space and time,
If only for a day.

Let me think that you were always mine,
It was always meant to be,
and put away all life before,
If only for an hour.

Let me brush you with my unseen kiss,
and wrap myself around you.
Let me trace my essence on your lips,
and feel you in my soul.

Let me touch your mind and merge with you,
If only for a moment,
and forever feel that this was life,
and we lived it to the full.

Mary McManus, Blackburn, Lancashire

ENOUGH SAID

Sometimes it takes so many words
to make myself understood,
in saying this now, too much.

Perhaps with wisdom,
I'll use fewer words,
and give each one more thought.

Some people talk too much
and say nothing.
I want to say less
and mean more.

Sarah Smithson, Chorley, Lancashire

SENILITY

White hair and nodding head
Bent and weary, face is set
A frown of pain, a stubborn lip
Lines of life drawn long and deep

Memory fades, lost in the past
Confused, confusing day and night
Hours peopled from the mind
Of days long gone in mists of time

The hours stretch in empty gaze
With nothing seen 'cept memory's pain
Lover lost and children grown
Gone long since with passion's throe

The daylight fades, the sun now sets
On years of life, love, work and rest
The person that we knew is gone
Claimed by aged childhood's thrall.

Jean Emmett, Accrington, Lancashire

ONE TOO MANY

I drank a bottle of sherry last night, and now I'm
feeling rough,
one after another it went down so quick,
I couldn't get enough.
"I'll only have the one" I said. I've said it lots
before.
After a few more glasses, "Go on then, I'll just
have one more."
I got up and had a dance, round and round the
table.
Another hour and some more to drink, then I
wasn't very able. I had no inhibitions, I didn't
have a care.
But my head was getting heavier, and my words
began to slur,
"Oh, I feel faint," I said. "I think I'm going to be
sick."
Slowly I staggered to the loo. "I think I'd better be
quick."
I don't think there'll be a next time, if there is
maybe I'll think twice.
My head has ached all today, and my belly's had
a pain.
How many times have I said this?
Never ... ever ... again.

Lynn Cooper, Bolton, Greater Manchester

WHAT IS IT LIKE TO BE DEAD?

What is it like to be dead?
Should death come swiftly silently on tiptoe
Or breathlessly in bed?
If there is pain how will I bear it and what will I regret
With the string of memories, sharp and wet?

Veronica R Emmott, Firswood, Greater Manchester

SILK

To a shop girl I requested
my approximate, size if I
were - like - a woman,
hypothetically speaking
you understand. A fourteen
maybe, or even a twelve
(if I lost a couple of pounds)
information is what I need,
that's all.

Janet Reger's catalogue of delight,
the sensuous caress of raw silk
clinging to my skin. Black lace
reflected in my dressing-table mirror
A basqued bandit in my boudoir.
Shimmering, secretive, seductive
thrills for no one to know.
Except me.

Geoff Mills, Oldham, Manchester

ENOUGH

He carried a bucket of rage, she a basket of
hand-me-down dreams.
She called them Love, regardless of Sylvia's
screaming.
She would adore her brute; his boots suited her
down to the ground.
From her heap on the floor, dreamed she could
love his sore, raw heart to healing,
Wished she could sweep away his dirt black
feeling,
Wanted to make it all OK
Though he dreamed up a new sin every day,
Just for her. Just for him, she took her penance,
sin sponge soaking,
Thinking she could suck up all the poison
without choking,
Hoping she could soak it up until they were pure.
He was her Holy Grail. This was a Holy War
Against the stark, dark death of dreaming.
'Cos he did it 'cos he loved her, he did it 'cos he
loved her
And she loved him 'cos he did it 'cos he loved her,
even more.
She believed. Nothing was ever enough.

Morag Reid, Birkenhead, Merseyside

AUTUMN

The trees look sad;
  And dry the leaves
    Like gentle tears,
      Fall -
Though the wind
  Kisses so softly
    Today,
As if to say,
  "Why weep,
    The time has come
      For sleep?"

Al Pearson, St Helens, Merseyside

ADLESTROP 2000

The station's gone. No train stops here.
A hiss of steam, a halting stop, then silence
when Edward Thomas heard one bird
joined by others, signature the sky.

It would have been a cherished memory
this English summer place in wartorn France,
the noise, the carnage, desecration.
There was no homecoming for him.

Today in large white letters
on a fox-brown metal board
ADLESTROP the station sign is seen
in the village bus shelter.

No one is here. I read his poem,
a plaque on the seat's back,
listen to the birds and watch the clouds
drifting in a timeless sky.

Fay Eagle, Prenton, Merseyside

THE BEDSIT

I hear a door opening and another one close,
A man's voice is bawling, at goodness who knows

The smell of the place is like old rotting bread.
Now the bed's knocking again, from the girl
overhead.

I'm fuming inside, at the price I am paying.
I've made up my mind, I'm definitely not staying.

If that chain's pulled again, I think I'll go mad.
I'm grieving I know for the home I once had
What a fool I have been, for a moment of love,
To give up a husband, for a man I now loathe.

A knock at the door, who will that be?
As nobody knows a nobody like me.
The boy next door is wishing me well,
And hopes I'll be happy, in this place just like
hell.

My bag's filled again, and once more I will roam,
And look for a place more like my own home.

Florence Bullen, Southport, Merseyside

ENVY

Envy is ...
Half a lager staring at a pint
A low fat cheesecakes view of a chocolate gateau
An independent single observing two lovers kiss
in a restaurant
A size 16 squeezing into a 10
A VW checking out a Porsche
A bedsit's longing for a penthouse suite
A Casio bleeping at a Rolex
A limerick comparing itself to an ode
Beige wanting to be blue
An ice cube clinging to an iceberg
A sparrow challenging an eagle
A poet eyeing up an anthology
Envy is ...
my inspiration

Michelle Wright, Oxton, Merseyside

North East

SACRIFICE

Garlands hang around her neck
In unsuspecting clusters clicking
and posing for pictures on the lawn
where the handshaking vicar
smiles and tries to look holy.

From time to time a shadow
crosses the sun and bright new clothes
are momentarily drained of colour.

In the village hall the women work
in whispers arranging the feast
unfolding fine white linen cloth
along the trestle tables.

In the kitchen a fly buzzes then settles.
Dust dances in the beam of strangely angled
light.
The women pause and catching the sound
of bells in the distance quietly withdraw.

The fly crawls drunkenly
across the wedding meat.

Three drops of blood
speckle a clean white sheet.

Joanne Benford, Hartlepool, Cleveland

THE LIFE OF SUMMER

The birdsong at the break of dawn
The rising of the sun
The dew upon the garden lawn
A new day has begun

Butterflies awaken
Wings unfurling to the sun
Caterpillar coats forsaken
Their metamorphosis all done

The damsel flies are darting
Over sparkling summer streams
As the fringe of reeds now parting
Reveal mallards' slumbering dreams

Swooping swifts gather insects
To feed their starving brood
The kingfisher from a branch inspects
Deep pools for silvery food

The balmy breeze of hazy days
Caresses our sun kissed skin
As winter weary spirits are raised
Outside and within

Sue Ireland, Stockton-on-Tees, Cleveland

DANBY DALE

My love, look down:
Below a bird so tiny
That rises and falls upon thermals blue.
Let granite rock
On hillside top,
Stand proud above farms of stone;
Let masks of clumpen trees
Hide fields of patch, and stream,
Like cottage quilt of treasure there:
Of tatties and of turnip sweet
That lay in wait a silver plate;
And let Danby Dale her arms entwine
Liken to a cloak of greeny brown.
Look, my love, forevermore
Upon my Yorkshire Dale,
I beg you;
Please rest within my breath,
And let every breeze so gentle
Fall upon my breast.

Kevin Leadbitter, Middlesbrough, Cleveland

REALITY OR DREAM

A quiet country garden,
With a quiet country house,
In a quiet country village,
Just like a country mouse.

I dream of such tranquility,
I dream of time to spare,
I dream of peaceful days,
Of birdsong in the air.

Would I find the happiness
That I am dreaming of?
Would I settle in this world
And learn to turn the sod?

Without my friends around me,
Without the traffic's noise,
Without the stress and tension
Or the supermarket joy's.

Reality is different,
Would it work as I have seen?
The dream could be reality,
Or reality the dream!

Doris Green, Darlington, Durham

YOU

You're the morning sun that falls on my face
You're the angel's wing that moves with grace
You're the petal that holds the morning dew
You're the evening sky with its brilliant hue
You're the newborn babe in its father's arms
You're the loving embrace that soothes and calms
You're the first light fall of winter snow
You're the fireside's warm and welcome glow
You're the beautiful hills and valleys of land
You're the tender caress of a lover's hand
You're a gentle breeze on a summer's morn
You're children's laughter sweet and warm
You're all the beautiful things I see
You mean and you are the world to me.

Sharron Bates, Newton Aycliffe, Durham

CHAINS OF GOLD

We all have chains that bind us
That hold us in our place
Some people try to break them
Others wear them with good grace
Some people's chains are steel
That are broken with such ease
Not caring for each other,
Just loving who they please
Some people's chains are silk
They weave them every day
A rich tapestry of life
Forged in the games we play

The chains that we are making
Grow stronger every day
Stronger with our actions
Everything we do and say
The links that we are forging
Are made of love and trust
Never to be damaged
Never to flake and rust
These chains can never ever
Be broken bought or sold
These strong chains that bind us
Are made of pure gold

Derrick Hopper, Bishop Auckland, Durham

RAFFIA SANDALS

A shade better than black
(I dare say this now).
Luminous green clock,
a few shades further.
The futon is puffed like popcorn,
as if no one had ever sat upon it.

Ahead is a trembling void,
that the future must fill.
Gone is the rock-red terracotta
and oh to be reborn,
to stand
lamp-post tall
in those raffia sandals
wearing a smile
with a sugar-free jelly-like heart
and those raffia sandals,
blisters and yawns.
Invisibly

catching the wisp of cirrus
that passes your mouth
as I long to kiss it.

Joanne Thompson, Chester-le-Street, Durham

CAT NAP

Contented, she lies
In sun-dappled shade,
Jade eyes glazing in
Tranquil reverie,
Memory stirs of
Dancing butterflies
Unwisely teasing,
She, the vigilant
Watcher, waiting,
Then with springing paws,
Gracefully arching,
Leaps, a feline Fonteyn;
Now she sleeps, playtime done,
Languidly lying in the sun.

Margaret Brewster, Seaton Sluice, Northumberland

DODGY WORLD

Modern technology is here to stay,
The world is smaller, what can one say.
Signals bouncing off satellites,
Make one wonder, is all this right?
I think of days long gone by,
Happy times without a sigh,
No wireless, TV or mobile phone,
Thank God no talk of human clone,
Those carefree days are gone forever
Let's hope we don't get too damned clever.

W G Osborne, Berwick-upon-Tweed,
Northumberland

WHEN YOU'RE IN THE BATH

When you're in the bath I miss you,
You're all sleepy and warm and private,
I wish I was one of the bubbles.

You're standing up glistening wet,
And steamy eyed,
The water's slithering away, having the
Pleasure of meeting you,
I'm pleased for it.

I smile in expectance, the towel roughly,
And tenderly soak the rogue damp,
In between places where my hand has been.

Material slips on smooth arms,
As you bend a leg to lower a shoulder,
Your hips tilt.

Coming from warm shadows to my room,
I'll read to you,
And tell you I love you.

Chris Howorth, Newcastle, Tyne and Wear

CONQUERING TIME

They hang in prickled shells
green-hidden in dripping leaves,
the colour of enclosing year
beyond the reach of up-stretched hands.

Small boys take aim,
the branches shake and shiver.

Silently,
reluctantly,
leaves fall
while longed for treasure hangs defiant
clinging tenaciously
through yet one more
Autumn day.

Connie Coates, Sunderland, Tyne and Wear

LAVENDER

Evening, a garden
A quick child
and a steady woman
gather dry washing.

Cuffs and collars
touched briefly to telling lips,
pegs plucked,
patient shared folding,
stroking all down neat.

Later at table
Mischief speaks.
"Grandad,
Grandma kisses your shirts
in the garden!"

Fluster rises
"That's how I check that they're dry!"

He smiles,
his neck warm in his collar.
He has watched her kiss laundry before.

Sue Lozynsky, Bridlington, East Yorkshire

JOHNNY, YOU'RE LATE AGAIN

'Johnny, you're late again', his teacher sighed
'Your excuse this time, perhaps you'll confide
Was it a UFO sighting? Were you hit by falling
stars?
Or kidnapped by funny little men from Mars?

'Johnny, you're late again, tell me what kept you
away?
Was it an earthquake, a tornado or snowstorm
today?
Did you save a kitten, stuck high in a tree?
Or were you chased by a bull? Please enlighten
me!

'Johnny, you're late again, your excuses you
embroider well
Most convincingly told, so I must urge you to tell
What, on your journey to school, delayed you
today?
Was it an enormous elephant, barring your way?

'Johnny, you're late again, you must please tell
me now
I can wait no longer to hear what detained you,
and how.'
Johnny stood before his teacher, in fidgety state,
'Miss, it was nothing exciting - the bus was late!'

Mary Wood, Hull, East Yorkshire

PERFECT WORLD

When I have gone to another world.
When I've popped my clogs
And my toes have curled.
I'd like to come back in the form of a cat,
But I'd like some conditions with that fact,
For I want an owner just like me,
Someone who'll buy fresh fish for tea.
A fresh pork sandwich for my lunch,
I won't be greedy but that won't be brunch;
For I'd eat plain cat food at the start of my day,
When I'd get lots of hugs and love, then I'd play,
But an owner like me? Well what else can I say?
That situation would be purrrfect.

Susan Higgs, Thirsk, North Yorkshire

BEYOND SILENCE

Darkness will steal across the empty miles
Unaware my time with you has gone,
The memories borne by our last summer
Dispersing in a half-remembered song.

Yellowed leaves will slip through listless fingers
With a longing for life that used to be,
And far beyond the sight of human eye
Will be the place no earthly man could see.

The broken thread will drift as gossamer,
And for a fleeting moment should you hear
Whispered sadness for the untold parting
Deep in seclusion share my absent tear.

Persuasive thoughts will come to you my love,
Every pensive minute set you free,
Moving into twilight's perfumed solace
Fragmented dreams will die untouched by me.

Rosamund Hudson, York, North Yorkshire

JUST AN IDEA

We would sit on the bus,
My friend and I discussing mutuality.
I, an Indian, him a muslim.
We would walk on beaches,
Arguing how to harbour cordiality.
I, a Chinese, him of mixed blood.
We would sit in cafes, looking
around and see pale faces exchanging

ideas with those black, shiny looking lads and
girls,
We were all looking for ways to harmonise,
Those were our dreams when we were young,
Thirty something years have passed,
That spirit which I was part of is
flourishing in all corners, perhaps not in the
Whole word but in our little island.
It was a good idea for us who believed in it

Will this idea of ours materialise?
Only time will tell.

Sam Pullia, Sheffield, South Yorkshire

THE WAY TO TOUCH A STAR

Not knowing, is the way to touch a star.
Small and half empty you can believe
that across the field and up the hill
you could hold that white light
in cupped hands and believing that,
you never need to go there.
Never need to really try and touch it.

Taller and full of concepts you know
on top of the highest of high places,
even on a ladder, on a tower there
your hand would only shrivel
in cold and empty air and the stars
would seem further from you.
Worse, you know they most likely died
before our fingers learnt to point.

Tony Noon, Mexborough, South Yorkshire

THE SPARKLE OF THE EMPEROR'S NEW CLOTHES

The precious priceless sparkle
Of the sunshine on a dewdrop
In a cobweb in the mist
Sparkles too in the smallest kiss,
In the scent of sweet-pea flowers,
In the whisper of the trees,
In a walk in a shower,
In a symphony,
Sparkles in the magic
Of a blackbird's crystal song
In the still air of the evening,
In laughter, in a romp,
In a cuddle with the cat,
In the eyes of those we love,
In a mug of steaming tea,
In a chat, in a hug.

Truly precious, truly priceless, the sparkle that's
not bought.
But manmade glitter that blinds with dazzle?
Truly, that's worth nought.

Eileen Caiger Gray, Doncaster, South Yorkshire

OF THE SEA

Think of me when you walk through my arch of
bones,
A gateway to adorn, for this I wasn't born,
For I was of the sea, and in me was seen
such great wonder and beauty.

Have you ever heard a whale sing
And the strange sad sounds that came from this
great thing?
Did you hear my cries and think that there were
no tears, and only the sea could fill my eyes?
For I was of the sea where men came and had
power over me.

Could you know the pain, the gnawing cuts in
stinging salty sea,
Or see me split open like a giant tyre
with all my inner tubes covering the floor
like slimy rubber, for my blubber,
was more important to me?
For I was magnificent and once knew how sweet
it was to be free
When I was of the sea.

Susan C Bullman, Castleford, West Yorkshire

THE FIRST FEMINIST

Eve, innocent of theology, asked: What am I to
God?
Carelessly snapped like a twig from a rib-cage.
An after-thought.
Last port in the storm of male dissatisfaction.
Even a petty god could have been more sensitive,
But he cast me in the invidious role of
late-comer,

Creation's also-ran.
And what divine caprice planted that tree
So fair and accessible?
He made it sweet and irresistible,
Like the words of the talking snake he made,
And dangled full of speech and promise of male
power
Before me.

And what is God to me?
An unfair God to send me naked and voluptuous
To Adam,
Who strutted full of uxorious priapism
And blamed me like that,
For dining on fruit.

Richard Marshall, Keighley, West Yorkshire

WHITE LIES

Deep clouds descend in a mass of charcoal grey
My face pressed against the glass so cold
I wish I could have begged you to stay

Sea of anger thrusts into the bay
The lies I forgot that you once told
Deep clouds descend in a mass of charcoal grey

We fell in love a year ago today
How can your rain and my tears be so bold?
I wish I could have begged you to stay

It was in this room that we used to play
I now remove this bitter ring of gold
Deep clouds descend in a mass of charcoal grey

Against jagged black rocks swirls the sea spray
All I want is your strong hand to hold
I wish I could have begged you to stay

My thoughts are at sea, lost within the fray
You were the one with whom I longed to grow old
Deep clouds descend in a mass of charcoal grey
I wish I could have begged you to stay

Natalie Scott, Wakefield, West Yorkshire

PRETTY TALES

Ho! Those Pretty Tales you told.
How golden were the days
When you told those Pretty Tales.
Like the one that said "We shall marry, you and
I in the bye and bye."
Then there was another one that began with
"I love you, Only you!"
Ho! Those Pretty, Pretty Tales.
You played a tune that my heart heard.
But it was the spoken word.
Another one was "We shall have the child that
you desire."

The Pretty Tales you told -
Of them I would never tire.
We will be together in a cottage by the sea
You and me, you and me.
Ho! What Pretty Tales you told.
And as I close your book of Tales
I see the inner page I never saw before
And it reads "Fiction" for all to clearly see
Except me!
Ho! Those Pretty, not so Pretty Tales.

Doreen Brook, Bradford, West Yorkshire

THE OLD HOUSE

Curious to passers-by, all boarded up,
A huge brick house, its garden wild,
With knee-high bluebells, dandelions and grass,
And an old outhouse crammed with junk.

I wonder when the house declined,
And who once lived there long ago,
I picture them - Victorian style,
A man in black, his wife in lace,

Reclining gracefully in the shade,
While two small children, seen not heard,
Play silently beneath the trees,
And dance like elves in dappled sun.

But now, the house is derelict,
With broken windows, dusty rooms,
Perhaps a squatter there resides,
And jacks up in the silent gloom.

So, past to present, time has gone,
The cold reality hits home.
But in these ugly modern times
Imagination still lives on.

Miranda Wright, Leeds, West Yorkshire

SINGLES COLUMN

if you want
cinema visits,
trips to the theatre,
country walks or
love animals and brats
are vegetarian and
like holidays abroad;
forget me.

i'm strictly a
jeckyll and hyde boozer
who chain smokes and
drifts from pub to pub.
a hell raiser who
lives on the edge:
i need a woman
who drinks and smokes
like a man.

Alan Holdsworth, Menston, Ilkley, West Yorkshire

PLAYING MEDICINE MEN

Mumbling about incoherence,
it rained only to make you laugh.
I was only teasing.
With peyote eyelids
you count thousands of lizards
running under stones.
Ground down fingernails,
powdered head to toe,
I try to see your visions.
I ate some of your cacti
while lying with iguanas
watching the sky for aliens.
The paranoia is stalking you
and then you look back to find
It's always been me.
I drink anything you give me,
green, soaking it in,
introducing me to health.

Rachel Jones, Halifax, West Yorkshire

Wales

TO KNOW

I have just realised I am nothing
nothing in this universe.
We are as grains of sand, but,
to waken and know!
This is a profound revelation -
a setting free.
Now I feel the world -
Know how precious it is.
As I look at this world with the
wind on my face,
tears dim my view.

Patience Musk, Ruthin, Denbighshire, Wales

POPPIES

Poppies of red among the grass,
Upright, stemmed heads, warm, glowing mass.

Calmly swaying in summer breeze,
Eighty years screaming, across Time's seas.

On Flander's fields they lay, crushed flat,
For soldiers' bodies, a soft red mat.

Grasses stained red, as wounds oozed blood,
Dead upon dead, cut down in bud.

Flowers of youth, a generation,
Fighting for truth, show veneration.

In foreign land, the ruled-straight rows
Of crosses stand, for all tomorrows

On lush, green grass of farmer's field
To testify, that they did not yield.

Between the spaces, growing pervading,
In holy places, small plant invading.

Territorial, blue, flower dot,
In memorium - forget-me-not.

Gwyne Carnell, Pontypool, Wales

REFLECTIONS

Sticky dark brown liquid
dribbles
unchecked over stiff grey
stubble
open mouth sucks
greedily
seeking every precious drop
vacant eyes stare
unseeing
into the corner shop window
reflecting
in his swaying
image
a hidden life
consumed.

Maggie Smith, Usk, Gwent, Wales

SIGHING WEARY

I am weary, sighing weary of you now;
Bowed, heavy head nodding-tired.
Bored drifting thoughts, once captured,
Replace emotions fuelled, stoked and fired.

Vibrant images that infused every second
Have, unnoticed, vacated my mind.
And my selfish heart has shrugged you off;
Its thrill of you long left behind.

Familiarity and time have made strangers
Of us, who turned and burned sleepless.
Loving and laughing in loud blazing colour;
To each other today, dull and lifeless.

I'm sleepy-sluggish in your company,
Those sparkly connections shut down,
Our togetherness leaden and stumbling;
Yes, I'm sighing weary of you now.

Karen Watkins, Carmarthen, Wales

STORY TIME

I have seen my father
in photos and rage.
Neither suit him.
It is the silent
concentrated gathering
of thoughts, belied
by inwardly roving eyes
that credit him most.

Expectantly waiting,
fixing him with gaze,
I witness a stare
that spans further
than any reach.
His mustered words
bring youth's eagerness
flooding back to my eyes.

Matthew Plumb, Abergavenny, Wales

WINTER AT LLNGRANOG

The gossamer threads of sunlight have split the
icy husks of night
And broke open the day.
The wind breathes new life into the chequered
green fields,
Rolling and caressing,
Like the quiet salt-sea sound of pebbles
Murmuring in the washing wake.
Clouds blown in,
Tumble down the skyline,
Draping and shrouding the land in a watercolour
mist.
The cliffs,
Dagger sharp,
Cut the foaming waves.
The spume bubbles in rage and dies.
I sat here as a young man, forty winters gone.
My new bride laughing with the sea, careless and
free.
I sense her in the blowing wind, she is with me
here.
The nurse turns my wheelchair to the bus and
snuffs out my living.

Michael Dalton, Bridgend, Wales

MY ANGEL OF PEACE

Each day the savage symphony continued;
The sun, snatching the baton from the moon,
Pierced my ears with screaming gulls
And crashing waves
Grinding the sand into submission.

Inland the city pounded its rhythm
To a counterpoint of the traffic's scream
Backed by mountains throwing up
Thunder cracks amongst wailing winds
Until nightfall when the baton was returned
To the moon

Even in slumber there was no rest.

Then two sweet bells chimed
And a new door was opened

I saw your smile and my world was silent.

Rhys Morgan, Neath, Wales

GHOSTS AT CAERPHILLY CASTLE

Behind my escarpment, history.
Stones that almost speak, mystery.
Wooden walkway to the gate,
To meet a greeting or gruesome fate.

Listen to the thud and rattle,
Archers shouts and sounds of battle.
In the great hall an open fire,
Candle light and sound of lyre.

Mead and wine, the minstrels sing,
Glory to Llywelyn, our royal king.
If these stones could tell the story,
of battles gone and lists of glory.

Now the castle echoes sound,
Of visitors, all looking round.
Watching, listening, hoping to see,
The past, as then it used to be.
Enthralled, they stare as in a trance,
And see the ghosts, in misty dance.

Gwyneth Pritchard, Caerphilly, Wales

THE NIGHT THE MOON DIED
(Lunar eclipse 9th January 2001)

Floating like a milky pearl,
swathed in silver strands of light,
tinged with pink and blue, my moon, my moon,
on that still and frosty winter's night.
A shadow spread across its face,
a dimming mask to hide its grace.
I watched in awe, my ethereal friend,
slowly turn from yellow to red, brick red,
it was almost as though,
the man in the moon was dead.
The world was darker with no moon glow light,
brighter, brighter, the stars that night,
that moonstone part of me deep inside,
felt my tears flow cold as I cried,
on that eerie, mystical, moonstruck night,
when I thought the man in the moon had died.

Gerald D Williams, Cardigan, Wales

THE RIVER

The wind blew softly the last time.
Then we were together and fed the bold
and noisy ducks, feeling as immutable
as the river but the river still flows
and now I walk alone.

The weak sun finds a small crack
in the wintry, grey-stained sky
and the iridescent water changes to
a dazzling yellow before more clouds come

slashing rain into the pregnant river.
It gushes angrily, a silvery-brown fiend
which bursts its banks, threatening
to excrete slimy sludge into nearby homes.

The river has a wild beauty today
but I'm lost in a summer far away.

Guy Fletcher, Pantmawr, Cardiff, Wales

Northern Ireland

SLATE

It is dark and grey and obvious,
This room.
Drum of April rain,
heavier with each fall.
The middle of afternoon
and I cannot see to read,
only free to stare at lead slates,
gazing at the church roof's waterfall
by streetlight.
This hemisphere rarely shines
on dull inhabitants
who score up the roads
or mould onto houses.
If only throughout the week
the sun would fix its course
and lift up the existence
of a shadowed land.

Colin Dardis, Cookstown, Northern Ireland

THE ANGELS OF BEN BARRA

In the delicate woods of spring
Bright with battalions of bluebells.
I can hear the forest breathing
Like the wings of distant angels.

From the west comes a slender wind
Where Ben Barra troubles the sky,
Emerald and Sapphire sequinned
Where the sun's golden legions lie.

Here I can see Erin's threshold
And the shadowy marble seas,
Lapping low as beauty unfolds
A fragile haze among the trees.

And here whilst young, they stood dreaming.
Robed in mist that the dawn expels,
And now only their soft haunting
Like the wings of distant angels.

Martin Magee, Craigavon, Northern Ireland

THE JOURNEY

Deep ravine of dark despair
Time moves slowly
Walking in the misty valley
clouded thoughts none to care

Time gathers speed
Mountain's foot is drawing nearer
Star of light becoming clearer
Time to take the challenge

The highest peak lies waiting
for me to start the rugged climb
Time moves on
Sitting on the grassy plateau now
sunshine bathes the dark ravine.

Hazel Wilson, Dundonald, Northern Ireland

OASIS

The bus is patched up, it is time to go.
I wait in the shade of a dust-drooped fig,
and drain the dregs of flat, tepid Fanta
from a plastic bottle.

A goat grazes in the branches
of a twisted tree.

The oiled reek of fried eggs
layers with rancid leather,
crushed herbs, spices from the East,
and camel dung swarmed with black flies.

The tin roof of the inn ripples with the rage
of the tubby Turk at Pat and Mick
about the drinks ordered by the Berber girls
who danced for them with tattooed thighs.

The door is blocked by the blue Atlas
of a Touareg, hand on the jewelled hilt
of his curved dagger, bladed with the shard
of a World War Two aeroplane.

The bus driver shrugs
and lights a French cigarette.

Noel Lindsay, Ballycastle, Northern Ireland

IT COULD ONLY HAPPEN IN IRELAND

The nun walked on uncertainly
Her long black skirt hampering.
She was no longer young and all her thoughts
On heavenly things concentrating.

The workmen on the building site
Saw her there but did not heed.
She lived in a different world from them,
Spoke a language they couldn't read.

She caught her foot against a stone,
Fell right flat upon her back.
Two men climbed down and forward ran,
When the foreman shouted; "Be careful, Dan
You really mustn't touch the maid.
Remember she's consecrated. Use a spade."

Beatrice Wilson, Holywood, Northern Ireland

NOT TOO BAD

Rough it smoothly, read the ad
above a Satisfaction Guarantee.
Now there's how life should be led
if an arrangement could be made:
nothing happening too uncomfortably,
the blow of Fortune just a gentle slap,
the slings half-strength, the arrows not too keen;
even a bad break not too bad,
leaving a fairly easy red
and, if not the rub of green,
at least the run of the nap;
a clause whereby the darkly sad
would be lightened a shade
to peace of mind dove grey,
with pain or rain not quite enough
to interrupt the play.
Yes, I'd like well balanced smooth and rough
on even-handed scales,
no bed or roses or of nails,
and the dream of a whiteish Christmas.

Noel Spence, Comber, Northern Ireland

Scotland

THE BAR

Full of people the place was alive.

Hamish propped up the bar
The alcohol diluting his blood further
Till he was Scotch.

Julio was in the corner
His latin charms oozing out
The girls flowing towards him.

The flashing lights surrounded Danny
The barrels spinning round and round
The coins pouring out.

She entered a silent bar
Encapsulating her new audience
The only sound her stiletto heels.

Wayne danced the night away
The music echoed in his soul
Alone, but dancing.

She glanced towards Julio
His eyes invited her over
She turned and left.

Laura McLeod, Brechin, Angus, Scotland

ST ANDREW'S HARBOUR

Midnight at the Kinness Burn
eiders ride at anchor and a ghost
heron stalks his own reflection
creel boats jostle at the pier
the ebbtide chuckles round their bows

I fold this vision inward
and seal it against time
that heron who has speared the moon
and swallowed a piece of silver

Kirk Saunders, Inverness, Scotland

ODE TO A GARDEN ON THE MARYHILL ROAD

Cars stream past
spraying exhaust gasoline
on your sparse little patch
of mean grass struggling
to keep clean.

Your old trees sighs
bowing beneath leaden skies
while on the branches
hung high
shimmers a painted
butterfly

Glass eyed squirrels, tails
Bristling bestride your ground
awash with gnomes
fishing forever around
your wishing well
of hope profound.

Theresa O'Hare, Bearsden, Glasgow, Scotland

THE DIY SEARCH

One moment of madness
On a young day,
In a young world
And someone demolished my paper thin walls of
self confidence,
Built flimsily with balsa wood of inner anxiety,
And held together with dry spit.
With a badly mixed cement of tension and fear;
For years I searched for supplies,
With no success,
But now I've built my own with the help of a DIY
store
Called Patience, Times and Son.

Ian Speirs, Kilmarnock, Ayrshire, Scotland

MY GARDEN

Lean flames leaped like locusts
this evening
in my garden.

Now from my bedroom window I must watch
bloodshot embers glare malignantly by night.
Beyond, black forests block out light
and the staring moon is blank and dumb and
blind.

I walk again at dawn
in my garden.
Ashes, grey ashes are my beautiful garden
and blistered fingers claw
the stony sky
where my tree was green.

They are all dead who lived here
in my garden.
I squat
and sift bleak cinders through bone hands.

Jack Hastie, Hilbarchan, Renfrewshire, Scotland

A WARTIME BURIAL

I buried Joey under green veneer
Of thinning grass surrounding London flats
In soil compacted by our constant tread;
A handy soup spoon was my makeshift spade:
No one with me to mourn his sudden death.
He did not know the ways of war until
Its fatal blast had rocked him from his perch
Alone while we slept through the battered night
In fragile safety scattered from our home.
Survivors then, yet really victims too,
For we knew well what war was all about.
And there are no safe shelters for the mind.

Leslie George Saunders, Balerno, Edinburgh,
Scotland

PHIL'S VOTE

"I'll vote for anyone
who says I mustn't wash,"
announced the five-year-old.

"And lets me live in fields -
gives me ice-cream to eat
and nothing else ..."

Everyone laughed at Phil
and his Elysium.

But adults also vote
for those who will express
- they hope -
their dream of worlds
better than those they know.

May C MacKay, Insch, Aberdeenshire, Scotland

NIGHTIME

A cremola moon
smiles from her
star stable

Onto a world
pinpricked with light

Cities and fields
never sleep
even though the
Sun has gone
absent without leave

The night people
work, walk, make love

Nocturnal creatures
roam forest
and fenscape

Even dreams are
awake travelling
to magic places

The night is charcoal black
but never sleeps.

James Adams, Dundee, Scotland